*Dorneywood*

*The North Front*

# Dorneywood

## J.N.P. Watson

ROBERT HALE • LONDON

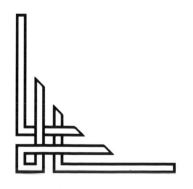

*© The Dorneywood Trust 1992*
*First published in Great Britain 1992*

ISBN 0 7090 5010 0 (paperback)
ISBN 0 7090 5069 0 (cased)

Robert Hale Limited
Clerkenwell House
Clerkenwell Green
London EC1R OHT

**Picture Credits**

Colour photographs by Mark Fiennes.
Black-and-white photographs on page 17 by courtesy of Mr Peregrine Palmer.
All others by Michael Chevis.

Design by Renaissance Communications, Dorking, Surrey
Set in Goudy

# Contents

**ERRATUM**
Foreword - page vii, line 14
'5th May, 1989' should read '5th May, 1980'

*Looking across the drive towards the North Front*

# *Foreword*

## By The Rt Hon. Viscount Whitelaw, CH, MC, PC

I count it a special privilege to contribute this foreword to the history of Dorneywood, because the house gave my wife and myself much pleasure and happiness in the nine years 1979-88.

It was a stroke of good fortune for us when Margaret Thatcher, as the new Prime Minister in 1979, offered me the house as Home Secretary. Our home was in my parliamentary constituency in Cumbria and there were weekends when my duties made it difficult for me to travel so far from London.

As a result, we were able to enjoy the peace and tranquillity of Dorneywood. Thanks to the excellent staff there, we entertained many guests both official and friends. We also have happy memories of family celebrations at Dorneywood, including our own fortieth wedding anniversary.

My wife and I found Dorneywood a welcoming house with a happy atmosphere, it also had the special advantage of surrounding country, fields and Burnham Beeches so close to London.

This made the residence particularly valuable for a Cabinet Minister who needed on occasions to be quickly available at the centre of Government. I shall never forget two such occasions. On Monday, 5th May, 1989, I had arranged an official lunch party at Dorneywood. The siege at the Iranian Embassy was reaching a climax. I decided that I should carry on with the lunch, as I could return very quickly to the Cabinet Office if required. As the lunch was about to start I was summoned urgently. Thanks to the superb driving of my driver, Jack Liddiard, and an excellent police escort, I reached the Cabinet office only nineteen minutes later.

In the summer of 1981 I arranged to stay at Dorneywood for the weekend after the riots in several cities. After a depressing and troubled week, I remember going back to Dorneywood and sitting out on the terrace on a most beautiful summer's evening; that gave me both comfort and encouragement.

It was experiences such as these which constantly reminded me of the value of Dorneywood as a residence for a Cabinet Minister. I also appreciated all the more the generosity of Lord Courtauld-Thomson in giving his cherished home for this purpose. My wife and I were also so grateful for all those who ran the Dorneywood Trust and the staff who cared for the house.

# Introduction

Crossing the Thames close to Windsor, driving north on to the M4, then travelling a short way westward, and leaving the motorway at exit 7, the visitor reaches Dorneywood from the south by crossing the A4 and wriggling his way though the built-up maze of Burnham village - once a sleepy hamlet, now a sprawling residential area that is part of the western suburbs of Slough. Then he strikes off from Burnham, in a north-easterly direction, along a mile of the quieter Dorneywood road; until, on his right, he arrives at the entrance to a brief drive, modestly marked by low chain fences and a sign proclaiming that he has found Dorneywood House.

Adjacent, to the north, lies the managed wilderness of Burnham Beeches, 400 acres of woodland, remarkable in particular for its massive, gnarled and distorted beech trees, their grotesque shapes being the result of more than three centuries of pollarding for fuel. That property has been owned since 1880 by the City of London (whose Sheriff and Lord Mayor enjoy by tradition, incidentally, a buffet lunch at Dorneywood each October on the occasion of their ceremonial planting of trees at the Beeches. One of the objects of the Dorneywood deed of gift was to protect Burnham Beeches from development on their south side).

Farnham Common and Farnham Royal are on the east side of Dorneywood while, immediately to the west, are the pockets of woodland and residential areas of Cookham and Taplow, now virtually all one with Maidenhead.

It makes an astounding comment on south-east England's bursting population - its urban development and ever burgeoning numbers of vehicles, requiring ever more and ever wider roads - that the whole general area between the Thames and Burnham Beeches, now almost all suburbia and dual carriageway, comprised, until about the time of the First World War, the Dorney farming estate which used to embrace the peaceful parishes of Dorney, Boveney and Burnham. Dorneywood farm, the upland sector of the old estate, contained its better drained pasture and the bulk of its woodland. Although a large proportion of the Dorneywood farmhouse (which forms the central structure of Dorneywood House) was not built until the twentieth century - on the site of one mostly burned down in 1910 - we felt it would be of interest for this narrative to convey impressions of the lives of the successive landowners, tenants and workers of the old Dorney estate, in the framework of some of the great events in English history, from Anglo-Saxon times to the nineteenth century.

However, the first landmark of outstanding significance in the story does not occur until 1919 when Sir Courtauld Thomson, as he then was, bought the lease of Dorneywood and its 250 acres from Charles Palmer, whose family had owned the Dorney estate for more than three centuries.

## Dorneywood

Courtauld Thomson (given his sure aesthetic eye and that of his artistic sister, Winifred, who lived there, too) promptly began to build on to, and to decorate, the house, and to fill it with the imposing wealth of treasures it still contains.  He was a man of such genius, of such towering ability, of such positive and boundless energy, and of such charity, that I have devoted a chapter of this essay to his life, giving some insight into his powerful and generous personality.   He was also enormously well liked (and was popularly known, among the more intimate of his host of friends, as 'Scorts', short for Sir Courtauld ).

The second landmark of outstanding significance falls in 1942 when Courtauld Thomson announced his intention to donate the estate to the nation, in particular to the incumbent Prime Minister;  to one of the Secretaries of State appointed by him;  or, failing them, to the Lord Mayor of London, or to the American Ambassador.   The title deeds were ceremonially handed over by the donor to the then Prime Minister, Winston Churchill, in the Cabinet room of 10 Downing Street.  Courtauld Thomson also offered to the nation the fifty-year lease of his flat with its contents at the Manor, Davies Street, to be the London residence of a Secretary of State.

As regards the description here of Dorneywood House and its contents, apart from my own appreciation, formed on a series of tours, I owe due credit to *Country Life*, and in particular to its two excellent articles written, in 1951, by Christopher Hussey, who was then the magazine's architectural consultant (having been its editor during the 1930s).   Also to Mr Jeremy Walters, who represents the solicitors, Charles Russell on the trusteeship;  and to Mr Leslie Croydon, secretary to Dorneywood Trust, for their unstinting kindness and assistance.

*The South Front*

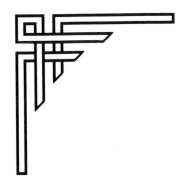
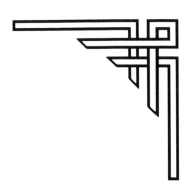

# Part One

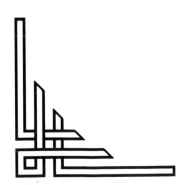

*The small dining-room*

# The Old Estate

## THANES AND VILLEINS

The name Dorney derives from the Old English word *dor*, a humble bee, the original Anglo-Saxon name being *Dorena Ieg*, the island of humble bees. For Dorney, four or five miles northwest along the Thames from Windsor, was - until the reclamation of the wet intervening stretch - an island, surrounded in winter by the waters of the Thames, in summer by marshland.

Dorney Wood, lying over well drained soil about four miles north of Dorney parish, close to Burnham Beeches, was the estate's upland farm - but contiguous with the rest. Until the twentieth century it was a simple journey to make from one end to the other, south to north, either by carriage or horseback or on foot. (But see the map now! Dorney village is separated from Dorneywood by the western sprawl of Burnham and suburban Slough, not to mention the M4. And the road journey through the conurbation is relatively complicated). In the old days Dorneywood provided some of the estate's best arable acres, its chief supplies of timber and firewood, its swine pannage and most wholesome pasturage. Although the stories of Dorney and Dorneywood were virtually combined until after the First World War this narrative will attempt to focus, where appropriate, more on the tract of Dorney Wood since it was on that land that the house which was to be allotted to a successsion of late twentieth-century Secretaries of State rose up. And that is our particular story.

This account begins some thousand years ago, with the first record of ownership. The name is Aldred, a thane and tenant of the Earl Morcar in the reign of Edward the Confessor, the last of

---

the Saxon kings in times when the feudal system and the land laws were still those of Alfred. Some thanes were landowners, some tenant farmers, some neither. But all of them, well horsed and well armed, served in the *fyrd*, or militia. It was through the thanes that the Anglo-Saxon lords claimed to guarantee the protection of all who worked the land. In those early times Dorney was worth three hides, a hide being the amount of land which could be ploughed in a year by one team of oxen - about 120 acres. Dorney's woodland was said to be sufficient for 150 swine.

Aldred would have provided his *churls*, or peasant labourers, with beasts and the ploughs and other tools to make a living; in return the *churls*, each allotted a 'yardland' of thirty acres, were obliged to contribute the best part of the produce to their masters. Their lives and those of their families were severe; their beasts and their meagre crops were their all; they lived in crude rectangular shacks of wattle and mud, rush roofs and earthen floors; they dressed in goat hair and unprocessed wool; they worked hard from dawn to dusk; and, when the harvest failed, they starved, famine being followed by pestilence. Life expectancy was short.

Rural existence being very essentially parochial and isolated, those rustics rarely, if ever, travelled; and the great events of England's Anglo-Saxon chronicles would have largely passed over the heads of both thanes and *churls*. The first firm impact that England's

changing tide of history would have had on the Dorney people would have been the invasion, in September 1066, by Duke William of Normandy, who claimed the English crown through his great-aunt, Edward the Confessor's Queen, Emma of Normandy. England's defence was undertaken by the brave and able Harold, whose father, Godwin, had been created Earl of the West Saxons by Canute. London - already the greatest and richest town and most important strategic site in the south of England, if not yet her capital - being little more than twenty miles from Dorney, news of the Norman incursion would have spread to the peasantry quick as wildfire. (Perhaps their thane had already ridden to join Harold's standard.) News, too, of Harold's advance northward to crush the invasion by another acquisitive cousin of his, Harald Hardrada, King of Norway, at Stamford Bridge; and of Harold's forced return march - broken only by forty eight hours rest in London - which culminated in his defeat and death at the hands of William's knights and bowmen at Hastings.

The people of Dorney were soon to learn of the unyielding and remorseless character of these Norman invaders, whose well-armed, well-mounted warriors had been hardened and fashioned in the stern school of repulsing the predatory Norse, Magyar and Saracen hordes from their homelands. William wasted no time, after his coronation in Westminster Abbey, on 25th December, in bringing Anglo-Saxon feudalism under royal control and giving the system the

harsher Norman character. The *churls* of
Dorney became, if not quite slaves, villeins or
serfs, who, if they deserted the land to which
they were tied by oath, could be brought back in
chains and brutally punished, under the jurisdic-
tion of the new *manoir* courts, which had
replaced the more easy-going Anglo-Saxon village courts.

William was also prompt to reward those who
had sailed with him, and their families, with
land. The Domesday Book shows Dorney under
the lordship of Miles Crispin with Ralf and
Roger de Anvers - sons of Roland de Anvers,
who had sailed with the Conqueror - as tenants.
Within a year or two of that the Danvers, as
they became known, were owners of those
estates. And the property was to remain in that
family until the second decade of the thirteenth
century. That is to say through the reigns of
William Rufus and good Henry I; through the
turbulent times of weak King Stephen and
Henry's formidable daughter, Matilda; all
through Henry II's long occupation of the
throne; all through his heated conflict with the
church; and the murder, instigated by him, of
Becket; through the time of that Henry's son by
Eleanor of Aquitaine, Richard Coeur de Lion,
and the third crusade which ended in Richard's
seizure of Acre and defeat of Saladin; through
his brother John's rule and the year the barons
forced that monarch to Runnymede to sign the
Magna Charta; through Henry III's half century
of power and the feud with Simon de Montfort;
and so into the reign of Edward I, famous for his
campaigns to subdue Scotland.

During the 1280's (a little while after Edward
made Wales an English possession by Statute of
Rhuddlan) the Dorney properties passed to one
William Cave. When a landholder died an
inquisition was held to give the king a record of
the man's estate and who his heir was, to ensure
that the feudal system was to be maintained and
the rights of tenure upheld, i.e. the hereditary

*The staircase, showing Rex Whistler's front porch mural*

rights, owed to both tenants and villeins, of feudal tenure. William Cave's inquisition recorded that eleven of his thirteen tenants were free men. One of the other two, the villeins, is referred to as follows :

'William Andrew holds half a virgate of land (or half a yardland, which would have been 15 acres) and pays yearly 16d and of other tallage 12d (the tax he paid to his landlord). And he ploughs and sows in winter half an acre of land and sows 40 half acres and this ploughing is valued at 4d. And he holds the same land and values it at 1d. And carries the lord's hay and that is worth 2d, and hoes the lord's corn for 1 day with 1 man and it is worth a ha'penny. And he ought to dig in the lord's curtilage for half a day and to pull a cart for half a day and all that work is worth 1d. And he mows 1 rood and half a meadow and makes hay thereon and it is worth 1d ha'penny. And he carts and stacks the lord's hay and it is worth 3d ha'penny. And he mows the lord's corn with one man for 8 days and it is worth16d. And he keeps at the lord's cost two men for one day at the lord's dinner and it is worth 2d'.

The Dorney peasant's working life would have become a little easier in the thirteenth century which saw great improvements in farming tools, in methods of estate management and in agriculture - composting, liming, seed experimentation and more effective breeding of livestock.

William Cave's son, Nicholas, inherited Dorney, aged fourteen, in 1300, and, remaining lord of the manor throughout the reign of Edward II, would have known of the King's horrific murder by torture in Berkeley Castle in 1327; would have gone on, too, to hear of the execution of the traitor Mortimer and the banishment of his paramour, Queen Isabella; of the early battles of the Hundred Years War (when taxes were levied more heavily on rural estates); and of the prowess of the Black Prince. During the thirteenth century and the first half of the fourteenth there was a considerable increase in England's peasant population. But, in 1348, came the Black Death when something between

one-third and a half of the population of the kingdom died of the plague within two years; and in general there was a shortage of men to till the land, while the price of labour went up at a bound. But it is uncertain to what extent that affected Dorney Manor. Anyhow, Nicholas Cave died in 1354 when a charter as to the inheritance of his kinswoman, Elizabeth Parker, and her husband, Thomas, referred to 'all the lands with meadows, pastures, rents and all appurtenances in the towns and territories of Burnham, Dorney and Boveney...'.

Nicholas Newenham, who acquired the manor in 1373, died six years later leaving it to his daughter, Clemencia, wife of John Paraunt, Serjeant-at-Arms of the King (Richard II). The growing spirit of rebellion surging through England's exploited working class during the 1370's came to a head in 1381 with the Peasants' Revolt. It was led by Wat Tyler, in a massive march that began in Kent and stopped at London's Smithfield - and was fomented by a statute geared to prevent the villeins and other labourers taking advantageous terms of employ-ment due to the scarcity of labour following the ravages of the Black Death - coupled with the imposition of a poll tax. Although Tyler's upris-ing was largely confined to Kent, Sussex, London and East Anglia, its repercussions at Dorney, given the national air of dissatisfaction, must have caused the Paraunts grave concern. There would doubtless have been an increase in outlaws, thirsty for revenge, keeping landlords on edge, men of the stamp of Robin Hood, whom upper-class justice had driven into the nearby forests, fastnesses such as Burnham Beeches. As for Dorney workers, their lot can only have been improved by the crisis. The feudal system was almost at its end.

The Paraunts, living during the illustrious reign of Henry V would have had news of the suppression of Wycliffe and the Lollards and may have joined in the celebrations following

*The tent room*

the King's triumphant march through France and his victory at Agincourt. One wonders, too, how many thanes from the vicinity of Burnham, Boveney and Dorney carried a long-bow or a sword, or trailed a pike in Henry V's army. A few years after Agincourt the Paraunts' heiress daughter, Elizabeth Carbonnel, sold the manor for £100 to a rich London baker, Thomas Scot, whose ownership lasted through the period of the Wars of the Roses. Richard Restwold bought the property's reversion from Scot's son, John ; and Thomas Lytton, in his turn, bought that from Restwold. So, on John Scot's death in 1505, Lytton became lord of the manor of Dorney. (He was the one who, about five years later, built the beautiful half timbered Dorney Court, which remains one of Britain's finest examples of an early Tudor manor-house).

According to the Close Rolls of 1510, Sir Reynold Bray had by then acquired the manorial rights and he was followed by his nephew, Edmund, who sold up, in 1529, to Richard Hill. The new owner appears to have been high-handed and extremely insensitive in his dealings with those under him. England had for centuries been the greatest exporter of wool in Europe and, that commodity being now of even greater importance, many landowners all over England were enclosing manorial land and evicting their tenants to make way for sheep. Hill was rash enough to have parts of Dorney Wood enclosed, a measure which produced a very angry reaction from his tenants and labourers. For the wood, so they claimed, was common land on which all those who had a stake in the estate were, by law and long tradition, permitted to graze their own animals. Hill hired six henchmen to guard the enclosures and keep the commoners at bay. And he went further than that. The Tudors' Star Chamber and court of Requests did much to check the abuses of enclosure and to protect the peasant against his landlord. And it was through the Star

Chamber Court that the tenants, represented by Thomas Woodford, appealed, in 1530, to Henry VIII:

'One Richard Hill gent and divers other ill disposed mischievous persons to your complainants unknown to the number of six persons the 10th day of March the 22nd year of your most noble reign did riotously forcibly and with force of arms that is to wit with bills bows staffs and swords and other weapons defensive and being arrayed and armed with harness and in the manner of war congregated and unlawfully assembled themselves at the said grounds called Dorney Wood and they and theirs with great force and violence by the commandment of the said Richard Hill did enclose the said grounds with great hedges quick set and deep ditches and did yet do threaten and menace your poor subjects to kill and slay them if any of them do or will claim or use their said commons in and upon the said premises by means of which enclosure threatening and other ill misdemeanours your subjects dare not nor yet can nor may use their said commons in the said grounds called Dorney Wood ... And the said Richard Hill not thus contented of his further malicious and wilful mind has edified one tenement in the said wood by occasion whereof divers arrant thieves by the sufferance of the said Richard Hill do resort to the ... house whereby divers of your subjects now of late have been robbed of their goods in passing by the said wood and divers beasts sheep and swine of your said subjects have been stolen and thereby conveyed away and sometime the legs of them have been cut off to their utter undoing'.

Hill replied that the Dorney Wood area in question was never common land but belonged absolutely to the lord of the manor and that he had every right to enclose it and to build a house there ('the edification of one tenement in the said wood'). This is the first mention of a building at Dorney Wood. Whether it is on, or close to, the site of the present Dorneywood House is not known . Hill insisted that there was no question of it being used as a thieves' den as Woodford and the other tenants accused, but by 'an honest true man to the knowledge of the said Richard Hill now dwells there and truly pays the rent thereof to the said Richard Hill'.

The dispute continued for five years. Whether or not it was ever resolved, Hill appears to have met his match in Thomas Woodford, who cut down a large oak on Dorney Green, insisting that was also common land. Hill, counter-claiming Dorney Green to be his, and his alone, sent his servants to cut up the tree and carry the wood to the manor-house. At the same time Woodford also dispatched a party of men to collect the timber, quoting a court held at the honour of Wallingford (to which Dorney was attached) as declaring that Dorney was a royal manor, and consequently that the Green was waste ground, common to all those living nearby. Meanwhile Woodford took revenge by teasing and harrying Hill's cattle with dogs. When Hill died, in 1540 - four years into the reign of the boy King, Edward VI - it was not surprising that his son and heir, John, promptly sold the estate. The man who bought it was a prosperous merchant, William Garrard, who was to become Sir William and Lord Mayor of London, in 1555 (a member of the same family, incidentally, that was to found the famous London silversmiths and jewellers). Hill's dispute reflects England's full emergence from the feudal system. By the era of Elizabeth I and that of Shakespeare, agrarian peace mostly prevailed, along with a high general level of prosperity, except in times of poor harvest.

The Dorney property went from Garrard to his son, another Sir William, in 1571; and from him to his son, Thomas, who got into trouble with a family called Clerck. Thomas Garrard, encouraged by the Clercks, wanted to marry their daughter, Dorothy, but his father objected on the grounds that Dorothy was older; but more, perhaps, as he put it, 'on account of the ill-disposition of the said Sir William Clerck' (Dorothy's father), who aimed, it seems, to get his hands on the Dorney estate, on which he

was later to buy a bond. After Sir William's death Thomas married Dorothy and then attempted to sell the property to pay the bond; but he failed to do so as his father had tied it up in trust. Thomas claimed that Sir William Clerck intended to 'sever him from his wife very soon after their marriage'.

The case went to Chancery at which Thomas's attorney pleaded that 'the said Sir William Clerck and his daughter were not yet contented herewith nor willing as yet to give over their covetous desires which they had to become absolute masters of your orator's estate'. The case having gone against Thomas Garrard and he being now estranged from Dorothy, who was living by herself in Dorney Court, he proceeded to try and reason with her parents. And they, according to the Chancery proceedings, 'started to revile him and told him that he should not live in his house nor with his wife any longer, nor would his wife live with him any longer'. Dorothy went further, sending Thomas word that 'if he lay in the street and starved he should not have a groat for his relief of her'.

Nevertheless, in 1616, Thomas took the case to Chancery again, and this time he won. The Garrard suzerainty of the Dorney properties came to an end in 1624, when it was decided to sell up. The purchasers were two brothers, Thomas and Richard Palmer, sons of a Kentish baronet. They kept the place in trust for their younger brother, James, who, in 1613, had married Thomas Garrard's sister, Martha. Sadly, Martha died, aged twenty-six, in 1617, giving birth to her third child, Henry. James Palmer's three small children were apparently looked after by their Garrard grandmother at Dorney Court, a house to which he had taken a great fancy.

## THE PALMER DYNASTY

For the next 300 years - about 1620-1920 - the Dorney, Burnham and Boveney lands were in the hands of the Palmer family (who hold the Dorney Court estate to this day). It was not until the mid-nineteenth century that Dorney Wood was treated as a separate entity. Owing to the Palmers' various political and religious proclivities and Royal connections during the seventeenth century the estate, and those whose lives depended upon it, ebbed and flowed dramatically between prosperity and dejection .

We have now passed from the age of the ruff and the farthingale to the lace collar and silk ribbon, the cavalier hat and ostrich feather and the bright colours of the Stuarts; while, on the land, the mud huts of old had mostly given way to yeomen's farmhouses and labourer's half-timbered cottages. The English farm-hand was, unlike his French and German counterpart, now essentialy a free man. And was, on the whole, well provided for.

During the latter years of James I's reign James Palmer, now in residence at Dorney Court, became a close friend of Charles, Prince of Wales, who, after his accession as Charles I, in 1625, knighted him with the appointment of Lord of the Bedchamber. Sir James was an art connoisseur (and quite a gifted artist too) and was largely instrumental in helping the king to build up his collection of pictures. Windsor Castle was less than an hour's ride from Dorney; and Whitehall, at least in summer, could be reached by coach in the day. So the lord of Dorney's absences from his estate on royal duty need rarely have been long. Following the death of his Garrard wife, Martha, he married a Catholic owning a substantial property in Montgomeryshire. She was the widow of Sir Robert Vaughan - Katharine, nee Herbert, by whom Sir James was to have six children. The Palmers were happy in the 1620's and 1630's and so were the royal family; and in general all was tranquil on the Dorney lands.

But the political storm was already brewing caused by Charles's fatal marriage to the French monarch's sister, Henrietta Maria, and his claim of divine right and absolutism, resulting in Parliament's frustration and anger. In 1641 the king sacrificed Lord Strafford who, as he was led to his execution on Tower Hill, was blessed from a Tower prison window by another of Charles's supporters, Archbishop Laud, himself on a charge of high treason. And all the time the disapproving faces of the Puritans, wearing their contrasting drab and severely cut clothes, were increasingly in evidence. Next came the King's attempt to impeach five leading members of the House of Commons. And the next few months were spent by him and Parliament in preparing their respective forces for battle. The thunderclouds finally broke in August 1642, when Charles raised his Standard at Nottingham, his

declaration of war. Meanwhile Sir James Palmer and his family, having placed Dorney in the hands of their steward, left for Montgomeryshire where Palmer had been putting together, at his own expense, a cavalry troop. The Dorney tenants were destined to suffer severely from their landlord's commitment to the Royalist cause.

The Parliament side, intent upon raising money, soon set up their Committee of Sequestration whereby landowners were required to yield large percentages of the values of their estates. When Palmer refused, Parliament ordered the Dorney tenants to pay their rents direct to the committee. And, for the next four years, the conflict dragged on - more and more in Parliament's favour. In 1645, the year of the Roundhead victory at Naseby - and, elsewhere, the near eclipse of the Royalist forces - Sir James was appointed, rather forlornly, Chancellor of the Order of the Garter. In the spring of that year a Roundhead troop rode over the Dorney lands and, being told of the valuables at the manor, broke in. The Speaker of the House of Commons then received a note from a senior officer on the subject, as follows;

> Yesterday in the afternoon having information that some troops had discovered at Dorney walled up in a private place some plate, money, linen and other goods to a considerable value which belongs to Sir James Palmer in actual war against the Parliament and at Oxford his lady if not himself a papist. Which troops by information were suspected to have gone from thence to get some more help to carry away the same either concealedly or to Wallingford caused me immediately to send out a party to seize and to bring into safe custody to this garrison for the use of the Parliament the said money and plate etc which was left in the possession of John Cotton (a bailiff formerly to Sir James Palmer) who lately upon security I released out of prison for going to Oxford [which capitulated three months later]; the party I sent out to Dorney returned to me last night with five loads of the said concealed goods consisting of many chairs, pictures, some bedding and other household lumber, but the money plate and linen (if there were any) will not be yet acknowledged...

Following the exonerating Articles of Oxford (1646) Sir James, who had spent some £7,000 in the Royalist cause, was able to return to Dorney Court; where, unsurprisingly, he found not only practically all his household goods removed but most of the manor's panelling torn down by Roundhead soldiers who had hoped to find money and other treasure there. Worse still his tenants had been rendered destitute by sequestration, heavy fines and other impositions, for which he submitted this petition:

> ... that he has been assessed for his 20th part at £1,000 in part where of one Mr Lawrence has received of his tenants of Dorney above £500 who have in billeting of soldiers and other taxes paid above the said £1,000 so assessed. Now in regard that these sums thus imposed upon your petitioner in so far beyond the proportion of his estate that by the several plunderings he has sustained during these wars he is not worth the £1,000 imposed upon him. And since he is comprehended within the Articles of Oxford which frees him from all the former 5th and 20th parts ... he humbly prays that his tenants at Dorney may not be pursued for their farther payments ...

Apart from the plight of the Dorney estate and its inhabitants, not to mention that of his own family, Sir James Palmer's last years were fraught with the tribulations of the second civil war, of 1648; the terrible news, in 1649, of his

*The dining hall*

friend's, the King's, execution; two-and-a-half years later - just about the time that Roger Palmer, Sir James's eldest son by his second marriage, was leaving Eton for Cambridge - of the invasion by the King's son, ending in defeat at the Battle of Worcester; and then the heavy-handed policing of Cromwell's major-generals.

When Sir James died, in 1657, it was 43-year-old Philip Palmer, issue of the Garrard marriage, who inherited the still crippled Dorney property. Philip was knighted a year after the Restoration,

but was more celebrated for producing at Dorney in 1665 (the year of the Great Plague) the first pineapple ever grown in the British Isles; and for making a present of it to Charles II (the event being recorded by Evelyn). Two years later Sir Philip was in serious trouble. Failing to come up with £11,000 owing on a surety he was threatened with confiscation of the estate. He therefore conveyed it, for the next five years, to his rich half-brother, Roger Palmer, Earl of Castlemaine, whose young career had been blighted by marriage to the notorious Barbara Villiers.

Roger became infatuated with that most famous of seventeenth-century beauties, the daughter of the 2nd Viscount Grandison, in 1656 just after he left Cambridge to start a legal apprenticeship at the Inner Temple. Barbara, not quite seventeen, was then already the mistress of Philip Stanhope, Earl of Chesterfield. However, Chesterfield being wanted for murder in 1657, and having fled to the Continent, she agreed to marry Roger. But his father was bitterly opposed to the idea. 'Sir James Palmer, having strong surmises of the misfortunes that would attend this match, wrote the contemporary historian, Abel Boyer, 'he used all the arguments that paternal affection could suggest to dissuade his son from prosecuting his suit...adding that, if he resolved to marry her, he foresaw he would be one of the most miserable men in the world'. That prophecy was not far from the truth.

Be that as it may, after Sir James died the following year Roger felt free to claim the girl of his choice; and, by virtue of having inherited the family's Montgomeryshire estate, sufficiently well-off for marriage, too. The wedding duly took place in London on 14 April 1659. And that, as his father foretold, was the start of Roger's great misfortune. General Monck having cleared the way for the collapse of the Commonwealth and for the homecoming of the true heir to the English throne, Charles II stepped ashore on 25 May 1660; four days later he entered the capital, The woman who the promiscuous new king chose to share his bed was the gorgeous, extravagant, witty, ambitious - and as unscrupulous and promiscuous as her Royal partner - 19-year-old Mrs Roger Palmer. Barbara was the one he slept with on his first night in London. To quote Marvell:

*In slashed doublet he came ashore*
*And dubbed poor Palmer's wife his royal whore.*

During the last couple of years of the Commonwealth Roger had been working for the Royalist underground movement. Whether or not Barbara Palmer had visited Charles in exile in Flanders and became his mistress then has been suggested, but not established. Anyway, she was firmly in that position from May 1660 onwards. Roger, now MP for Windsor and needing a London house took one in King Street, which - most conveniently for Mrs Palmer and the King - backed onto the privy garden of Whitehall Palace. The lovers were regularly witnessed together, and Pepys, who was at the Cockpit theatre in April 1661, noted in his diary that 'my pleasure was great to see ... so many beauties, but above all Mrs Palmer, with whom the King doth discover a great deal of familiarity'.

Following his marriage to the King of Portugal's daughter, Princess Catherine of Braganza, in 1662, Charles decided he wanted Barbara still closer; he was determined she should be a Lady of the Bedchamber. Having overcome Queen Catherine's furious opposition to that outrageous proposal, the next step necessary was to enoble Barbara which he did by creating Roger Earl of Castlemaine.

If one is to believe Evelyn and Marvell and Pepys (the appreciative eyes of the latter seemed to be following Barbara Castlemaine whenever the opportunity occurred) the subjects of the embarrassment of Dorney's landlord and the scandals of Dorney's chatelaine provided London's principal gossip, So what, one wonders, would all this have meant to those whose lives were spent in the villages and farmsteads of Burnham, Boveney and Dorney? The talk must have provoked a good deal of outrage and almost as much amusement.

Meanwhile, in February 1661, Barbara produced a daughter, Anne, who - although more likely to have been the King's (as all Barbara's subsequent babies almost certainly were) - Roger

Opposite: *Sir James Palmer*

Left centre: *Roger Palmer, Earl of Castlemaine by Sir Peter Lely*

Right centre: *Barbara Palmer, Countess of Castlemaine by Sir Peter Lely*

Bottom left: *Sir Charles Harcourt Palmer of Dorney (1760-1838)*

Bottom right: *Colonel Charles Palmer who sold Dorneywood to Sir Courtauld Thomson*

accepted as his own. (For celebration of her birth Roger and his half-brother, Philip - who, that year, was knighted and appointed Royal Cupbearer - had a new porch built on to Dorney Court's chapel with the date, 1661, inscribed above the door.) In the following year Barbara's second child, Charles, was born at the King Street house. Roger, who had by then declared his Catholicism, had the boy christened by a Catholic priest. Barbara had for long wanted to be rid of her husband and used this for her excuse (although, hypocritically, she herself became a Catholic convert at the end of 1663). With the King and the Countess of Suffolk as sponsors, she arranged a second baptism, an Anglican ceremony, the child being named Charles Palmer, Lord Limerick.

With that drama over Roger's wife leaves the Palmer story, her turbulent career continuing with several more heavily titled children; elevation to Duchess of Cleveland, in 1670; to be the mistress of John Churchill, the future Duke of Marlborough a year later; and - after Roger's death, a bigamous marriage to General 'Beau' Fielden which was duly annulled - to die aged sixty-eight, in 1709.

Roger had enjoyed a distinguished naval career with both the English and Venetian fleets in the Dutch wars. But as a Catholic, and, according to the evidence of the notoriously deceitful Titus Oates, a treacherous one, he spent nearly three months in the Tower in 1678-79; and again in November 1679. His star was in the ascendancy under Catholic James II who made him a Privy Councillor and ambassador to the Vatican. For that William and Mary, in their turn, had him arrested in Wales, in October 1689 (the charge was one of 'endeavouring to reconcile this kingdom to the see of Rome'). So he was committed to the Tower for a third stint, this time being released on bail in February 1690. He died at Welshpool on 21 July 1705, but not before being imprisoned twice

more on accusations of treason.

Twenty-three years before that (1672) Roger had resettled the Dorney estate on his impoverished half-brother, Sir Philip (a man some twenty years older than him). Sir Philip died in 1683 (the year of the abortive attempt to assassinate Charles II and the Duke of York on their way from Newmarket to London, the Rye House Plot). Philip's brother, Charles, now came into the property; and having no heir, married a distant cousin, Jane Jenyns, aged 16. It was their union that produced the present Palmer line, their eldest son, Charles, inheriting a week after the death of Queen Anne, in 1714. A few years into the reign of George II this lord of Dorney also inherited, through a cousin, the baronetcy of the Kentish Palmers. After his eldest son (by his marriage, in 1729, to Anne Harcourt) died, aged thirty-three, serving with a unit of the East India Company at Sumatra, their eldest son, Charles Harcourt Palmer, took over Dorney from his grandafther, and inherited the baronetcy in 1773.

The first evidence of a house on Dorney Wood farm was, as we have seen, in the sixteenth century, in Richard Hill's time. The next mention of one is during George III's reign, in 1782, when Sir Charles Harcourt Palmer granted a lease to William Neighbour, of Taplow, for an annual rent of £70 10s, the farmhouse being on the site of the present Dorneywood House. The Neighbours were followed in the leasehold by a family named Stannet. A document of 1841 makes the farm over to 'Elisha Stannet of Dorney Wood farmer for 21 years at £180 and £20 for every acre ploughed'.

Although Sir Charles Harcourt Palmer died unmarried, and the baronetcy became extinct, he had been living, more or less throughout his life, with a cousin called Caroline Bonin. One of their younger sons, Philip, farmed Dorney Wood, being described by his father in 1835 as

# Dorneywood

'Philip Palmer of Dorney Wood, farmer'. The lease by his elder brother John, of Dorney Court, worded it 'a messuage in Dorney Wood for £150 plus £20 for every acre of meadow ploughed'. But members of the Stannet family also still leased a part of the land until the 1850s.

John, having died without issue in 1852, his brother, the Revd. Henry Palmer, vicar of Dorney, came into the estate, and was at the helm until he died in 1865. Whereupon his son, Charles (born 1829) became owner. Between the 1860s and early 1890s Dorney Wood farmhouse was occupied by William Webster and his substantial family. Webster was the son of a local grain dealer and seedsman.

Following the departure of the Websters during the 1890s Dorney Wood farm was taken in hand by Charles Palmer, the Revd. Henry's heir. A little later he converted the farmhouse into a 'gentleman's residence', a manor-house. Shortly after the Victorian era phased into that of King Edward VII it is listed as 'Dorneywood House, the residence of Paget Toynbee'. When a fire destroyed part of the house in 1910, Toynbee went to live at another Dorney house, Five Ways. In 1919 the vicar's grandson, another Charles Palmer, sold Dorneywood House and the farm to Sir Courtauld Thomson, through whose beneficence the home became a national property and to whose career we now turn.

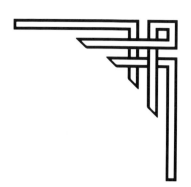

# Part Two

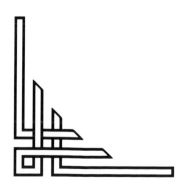

*Looking over the rose garden towards the house from the south-east*

# The National Legacy

## THE MAKING OF THE BENEFACTOR

The man who bought the lease of Dorneywood from the Palmers; who fashioned the house and its outbuildings and grounds into the beautiful features they are today; and who was, after thirty years or so, to give all that to the nation, displayed little scholastic intellect. And, notwithstanding Courtauld Thomson's superlative educational opportunities (according to the standards of the 1870s and 1880s) few people would have predicted, during his childhood and early youth, that he would one day become a business leader and charitable administrator of towering ability and influence. (It should be placed on record, however, that when he was four years old his father commented to his elder sister, Elspeth, that 'some day baby will be a great man in business').

That baby was born, the youngest of four children, in Edinburgh in 1865, into an ambience of upper-class affluence. His father, a considerable figure in mid-Victorian Edinburgh, who appears to have come into a great deal of money, was also a distinguished inventor. He created the first steam carriage, the first floating dock and an ingenious fountain pen; and, although J. B. Dunlop was the first to take out a commercially successful patent for the pneumatic tyre, Robert Thomson was the pioneer of that invention. As for Courtauld's mother, Clara (née Hertz) she was, by all accounts, a woman of great charm, good looks and competence, and of wide interests.

Why 'Courtauld'? The answer is that Samuel Courtauld (co-founder, with his brother, of the silk manufacturing firm) agreed to stand as godfather only on the condition that the child be given his surname for its christian name. Robert Thomson died when Courtauld was seven years old. Clara soon married again, this time to a barrister, John Fletcher Moulton. In general he proved to be a good stepfather, but one who, in due course, would give Courtauld a lot of trouble.

The boy's schooling began well enough with a pre-preparatory run by a Miss Dixon, with whom he enjoyed a happy rapport. But he didn't really like books and particularly disliked classical subjects. So at Summerfield (later called Summerfields), one of Britain's half-dozen best prep schools, an academy celebrated for the high number of scholarships it achieved to the leading public schools, he gave the impression of being a dunce. He duly passed, at a shamefully low grade, into Eton, where he was to board at

*The principal picture hanging in the drawing room at Dorneywood: A view of Eton College and Chapel seen through the gateway of the north terrace of Windsor Castle, 1856, by William Cowen. The house at which the schoolboy Courtauld Thomson boarded (Luxmoores's) is identified below the chapel*

H. E. Luxmoore's house (a housemaster well known to Etonian posterity for 'Luxmoore's garden') Throughout his life Courtauld relished grandeur and to rub shoulders with grand people, penchants first expressed in his (unpublished) memoir - the only mention there of fellow-Etonians being his two titled 'fagmasters' and a boy he stayed with in the holidays, who was also titled. He enjoyed Eton, partly because he was quite a prominent games player, in the days when prowess at games was highly prestigious at the public schools.

Meanwhile his work was going badly, and Luxmoore told his mother that, unless his handwriting improved, he must be expelled. So, in the holidays, he laboured long hours under an old-fashioned writing master, to return the following half with a hand his examiners could read. ('Unfortunately they then realized', recalls Courtauld, 'how inadequate my answers were to their questions'.) It was in vain that Fletcher Moulton wrote: 'I feel sure my boy will do his very best this half. Steady hard work at your time of life develops the mind ... So do your best, dear Court, and make both Mum and myself proud of you.'

Notwithstanding his poor results he was accepted for Magdalen College, Oxford. But, failing to pass the interim exams there he was informed he was to be sent down. His mother appealed to the president of Magdalen who wrote back that Courtauld was 'much above the average... in practical ability and judgement', and the tutorial board granted a reprieve. His biographer, L.A.G. Strong, attributes the ignominy of his academic career to the 'dead-hand' of the contemporary schooling tradition, which often failed to tap individual talent. It should be added that the then upper-class prejudice against commerce and trade, the principal subjects in which Courtauld was to excel, was reflected in the teaching. Knowing the factors, poor writing and difficulty with reading despite a good brain, one wonders, too, whether he wasn't slightly dyslexic? Anyhow, with his stepfather's influence he was now launched on a legal career, being enrolled as a student at the Inner Temple. However, although he got as far as scraping through the Roman Law exam, he soon parted company with that profession.

In view of a later connection with Dorneywood perhaps the most important contacts Courtauld made during his Inner Temple days were those with the Russells. 'The whole of the Russell family became very intimate friends of mine from that time,' he recalled. 'I often stayed with Lord Russell of Killowen [Lord Chief Justice, formerly Sir Charles Russell] at his Epsom home, and a more kind or helpful friend one could hardly hope to meet. His son, Sir Charles Russell, became a very famous solicitor and, although he is long since dead, his firm are still my solicitors.'

His first break came when he 'migrated to the West End', as he put it, 'where people looked less clever and less competitive'. During the year or two before his mother died, which was in 1888, he was in the habit of accompanying her on carriage expeditions to antique shops (she

was a collector of old china). And he so much disliked being bumped about by iron-clad wheels on ill-laid streets that he determined to design his own vehicles; and he did just that, so proving himself a 'chip off the old block'. Having found a coach factory he began manufacturing broughams without front seats, which he christened coupés, smart, light, well-sprung four-wheelers with pneumatic tyres. He was also off to a good start on the equestrian side of the business. Having enjoyed riding to hounds since boyhood he was a sound horsemaster, and he now had himself coached as a whip. Thus the manufacturing phase got underway with scarcely a hitch.

Courtauld no sooner had the coach venture going well, in 1889, than he was approached by a firm of financiers who, having bought an Alaskan gold mine, discovered that they had been severely defrauded. They were looking for a young man with some knowledge of law who would, for a modest fee, travel to the site and see if some of the money might be recovered. Fletcher Moulton, who himself had invested in the mine, suggested his stepson. Once Courtauld had his coach business squarely in the hands of a reliable manager, he crossed to New York and travelled, by train, to San Francisco. There the solicitors representing the financiers advised him to make the journey to Alaska with a detective called Davis, who in his turn persuaded his charge to pose as a mental patient since any Englishman seen in Alaska at that time of year would be bound to arouse suspicion. (Especially, added Davis, one dressed in such a bizarre fashion as Courtauld.)

The railroad being snowed up they had an appalling journey to Victoria, Alaska, by sea (in what Courtauld described as an 'ill-found, over-crowded tramp steamer'). From there they set off for their Alaskan island where they were quick to discover that the so-called mine had been 'salted' with samples from a genuine nearby

*Courtauld Thomson in early manhood (artist unknown)*

*The logo for Courtauld's coaching enterprise*

mine (that is to say that samples from the genuine mine had been substituted for some from the worthless mine). At this juncture, while Davis continued the investigation, Courtauld went down with a devastating attack of pneumonia. He became so weak and feverish after a few days that, when Davis asked if there was anything he particularly wanted, he just whispered two words - 'the fish'. He referred to a little wooden token of which he had already spoken with animation to Davis. An Indian witch doctor wore it on his wrist and Courtauld was convinced of its healing power. Davis, having secured the treasured talisman, folded it into the feverish hand and, from that moment, the patient began to recover. ('I often asked Davis how he got the fish,' recalled Courtauld, 'but he always replied "you must never ask!'. He and Davis then soon had the knots of the mining racket unravelled, and wasted no time in returning to San Francisco to report to the solicitors.

Courtauld was back in London early in 1890. The coupé manager having discharged his duties with due credit, a splendid fleet of Thomson broughams started business on 1st May 1890. 'The coachwork was highly varnished,' he wrote '... the inside was upholstered in dark blue leather and cloth, with cushions of the same material ... The harness was beautifully dubbed and polished. To complete the turnout the coachmen were dressed in white breeches, top boots with turn-down leather tops and high silk hats ... '. And, with Courtauld back in charge, as many as 200 orders a day had to be turned down. ('I took to business,' he related at the end of his life, 'as a duck takes to water.') But, when a little later, the horseless carriage came on the market intuition told him that his enterprise had seen its best days. He therefore sold it to the Dunlop Tyre Company (who wanted to try further experiments on the pneumatic project). He put a measure of his capital gain into building and went on - among many other pro-

jects - to build Mayfair's first block of flats and to contract to replace the Old Bailey with the Central Criminal Court.

After their mother's death Courtauld and his two sisters very much led their own lives. Elspeth married the author Kenneth Grahame, while Courtauld and the intelligent and artistic Winifred set up house together in London at 59 Pont Street, which was to be their London base for forty years. Neither of them ever married. Courtauld had been quite bitter about his treatment after the Alaskan adventure. 'I went to America for nearly a year on a very difficult and dangerous piece of work for him [Fletcher Moulton],' he complained, 'for which I never received any payment'. Nor was that the only instance of his barrister stepfather's failure of integrity. Courtauld and the two sisters were obliged to sue him over their mother's will, which, significantly, was all in Fletcher Moulton's handwriting. (The other son, Harold, was apparently well provided for.) The case being heard in April and May 1905, the judge found both parties in the wrong, since neither had kept accounts. The Thomsons' appeal came before the Master of the Rolls, who decided in their favour. Fletcher Moulton settled his account with his stepchildren and resigned from the trusteeship. (The adverse publicity of the case, however, did not prevent him from becoming a Judge of the Court of Appeal.)

By the time of that trial Courtauld held a large number of lucrative directorships and, in 1912, was knighted. In 1913 he and Winifred had just returned from Bengal, where they attended the Durbar as guests of the Governor, when he was offered and accepted partnership in a highly successful antiques reproduction firm and also the chairmanship of the Goldsmiths' and Silversmiths' Company. He was now a very big name in the city. There was an air of efficiency and meticulous dealings in all he did. When recalling his American adventure he

*Christmas cards drawn by Tenniel for Courtauld Thomson and his sisters between 1893-98*

*Looking over the Dell towards the conference room*

makes the following significant comment: 'In connection with Chicago merchants I am reminded of a book written about that time, *A Chicago Merchant's Letters to his Son*. There was a phrase in one of the letters: "It does not follow that a man in a clean shirt is clean underneath, but he is more likely to be clean than a man in a dirty shirt." In life I have generally found that an organisation that is efficient on the surface is more likely to be well managed than one that is inefficient on the surface.' A simple and obvious statement, perhaps, but one containing a principle often ignored in practice.

Towards the end of the summer of 1914 he rented the Corner House at Gullane, in East Lothian (which he was to do again, annually, once the war was over; and where, incidentally, at the nearby golf-course of that name - whose president he was to become - he was well known as an energetic and able player). Sir Charles Russell, who was staying with Courtauld there, sought his advice on how best to use the numerous works of art that had been donated to the Red Cross for the war effort. Courtauld replied: 'Have them auctioned at Christies.' Within a week or two he found himself chairman of the appeals committee; and not long after that - given his reputation as an organizer of exceptional ability - he was appointed Red Cross Commissioner (unpaid, but in the rank of colonel), first in France, then in the Middle East. Colonel Sir Courtauld Thomson spent practically the whole war abroad, frequently living in very rough conditions; frequently, too, in close physical danger. He was appointed Commander of the Order of the Bath in 1916. His letters to Winifred demonstrate his great humanitarian qualities. 'I have been in every hospital in Malta, Port Said, Cairo and Alexandria,' he was, for example, writing from Cairo in June 1915;

> ... and have traced the wounded back to the source at the front, where I saw the men taken from the trenches. I have travelled with the wounded as

they were taken on barges from the beach and then on with them in minesweepers to their hospital ships. The sights I have seen are staggering in their awfulness. At home one gets in the way of looking on a wounded man as something rather interesting with his left arm in a sling or a neat bandage round his head taking tea with ladies, but when you see them straight out of the trenches it is more like something in a slaughter-house. The courage of these lads when they go into action is only equalled by the courage with which they stand the agony of their wounds ...

After his hospital ship had been under heavy fire from the Turks during the Dardenelles campaign he wrote:

> I got hold of 4 or 5 padres who were on board and 3 or 4 officers who were slightly wounded and we placed ourselves under the orders of the medical officer in command as orderlies. He asked us first to get the men out of their clothes, wash them and put them in the clean pyjamas and shirts I had brought with me ... I will only tell you of one poor boy who was shot through both eyes ... I noticed he never asked for anything not even water tho' of course they all suffered from intense thirst ... When we got to Alexandria I told him we were getting alongside and I saw his hand moving about trying to find some hing. I asked him what he wanted. He said simply 'I want your hand.' When he had taken it he held it a minute and then went on: 'Please tell me your name, you have been very kind to me.' It was really a minute or two before I could answer ...

Within three weeks of the Armistice Colonel Sir Courtauld Thomson wrote to Winifred that he had 'told Charles Russell to buy the lease of Dorney House ...'

> ... Of course in one sense it is putting one's head in a noose as regards the owner as he will think I am bound to buy the freehold at his own terms ... I ought to be home by the spring and we might get the use of it for the spring and early summer ... I feel I could do with a little reposo. The strenuous time still goes on. I hope you will like Dorney House if I get it. It could be quite charming but has many defects as it is.

It was not long before had had grown to love the

*A charcoal drawing of Sir Courtauld by Sargent in 1910*

*Lord Courtauld-Thomson (left), sitting opposite his sister, Winifred, with some of their young Commonwealth guests during the Second World War. He had then recently been created a peer*

house and to buy that freehold. And he continued to grow, between the wars, in public influence and esteem. His immense work for hospitals which began as a committee member of the new King Edward VII's at Midhurst, Sussex, in 1902, and continued through the First World War, expanded enormously during the 1920s and 1930s (see *Who's Who* entry, Appx A). Before the start of the Second World War Courtauld was on the board of no fewer than thirty companies, besides holding such honorary posts as Chairman of Brooks's Club. His industry and iron discipline, coupled with his imperturbability and kindness, were a national byword. He was an inveterate traveller, and, being a very gregarious and social man he was,

too, a huge entertainer. 'Friendship and cultivating the society of those he liked and admired', comments Strong, 'were the chief pleasures his life afforded.'

The Second World War saw septuagenarian Sir Courtauld Thomson as the Red Cross sales director and chairman of the Lord Mayor's Red Cross and St John's Fund. From September 1940, Dorneywood House (as it was now known) became celebrated as a leisure retreat for officers of the Commonwealth armed services - with himself and Winifred as the much-loved hosts. His intention to leave the house to the nation was first mentioned in a letter to Elspeth in 1942: 'I hope to see Ld Portal soon about my offer of Dorneywood etc. I should take an even greater interest in it if I knew it was to be preserved for the nation.' The gift - as a retreat for the Prime Minister or one of the Secretaries of State - was announced in *The Times* on 21 April 1943. Meticulous Courtauld even stipulated an expenditure list for whoever the incumbent might be '... not with any idea of limiting the resident's expenditure, but rather to indicate to him my desire that he should entertain on an ample and hospitable basis ...'. Courtauld was awarded a peerage, taking his seat as Lord Courtauld-Thomson on 9 February 1944.

The *Evening Standard* celebrated his eighty-fifth birthday by remarking that he 'breakfasts at eight, is at work in the office of his flat by nine and thinks he is returning early if he is back at home by ten-thirty in the evening ... He can still play an eighteen-hole round of golf, he watches football, boxing and skating and does not wear an overcoat'. If Courtauld was to have named one favourite charitable work it would doubtless have been his chairmanship of the King Edward VII's hospital at Midhurst, which he had held since 1923, and to which he devoted an extra special proportion of his generosity and thoughtfulness. It was there, too, that he died, aged eighty-nine, on 1 November 1954.

*A cartoon of appreciation sent by one of the Commonwealth air force Officers*

*The conference room*

## DORNEYWOOD HOUSE

Let us now take up the thread from the conclusion of the first paragraph of my introduction, that point at which the visitor reached the drive entrance. He proceeds along the brief drive, which is flanked by saddle-stones; and, having parked in the forecourt, he turns towards the white front door which marks the centre of the north face of the house (p. vi).

In terms of proportions Dorneywood, both outside and in, still has the general character less of a stately home than of the Georgian farmhouse it originally was. Yet it is somewhat larger than that for, in 1920, Courtauld Thomson added an east wing. To eliminate the draught he also had an inner porch constructed; and, from that, he had created one of the most beautiful features of the house. Impressed by Rex Whistler's murals in the Tate Gallery dining-room he commissioned the young artist (then living nearby at Farnham Royal) to paint a picture to cover the bland surface of the porch's back wall' and the subject Whistler chose was a romantic image of the Goddess Flora and Cupid visiting Dorneywood (p. 6).

A thank-you letter from Whistler, also held at the house, carries a comic sketch of Lord Southborough unveiling the Oswald Birley portrait of Courtauld Thomson at the presentation ceremony. While on the subject of comic sketches there is a delightful set by an old friend of the Thomson family, Sir John Tenniel, the *Punch* cartoonist and illustrator of *Alice in Wonderland*, who was in the habit of sending amusing drawings each New Year to Winifred Thomson and her sister, Elspeth (Mrs Kenneth Grahame) when they were children in Edinburgh (p. 28).

The Birley portrait hangs in the hall (p. 36).

Anyhow, in Courtauld Thomson's day, the function of this large entrance room was entirely that of a comfortable hall, and a most decorative one it was, too; but, with the advent of the resident politicians, who would sometimes need to entertain on a larger scale, a substantial dining-room table was put in there, along with an appropriate number of chairs (p. 15). Just beyond, to the right, the room that was Courtauld Thomson's little library is now used as a dining-room by the resident family and their house guests (p. 2).

Turning left from the front door through the hall is, firstly, the study (formerly Courtauld Thomson's dining-room) with, over the fireplace, a landscape of Cassis, donated by its artist, Winston Churchill, as an addition to the gift of Dorneywood to the nation (p. 37). Among its other treasures this compact room contains a Pembroke table with what Courtauld Thomson called 'five-minute books', books in which someone with five minutes or so to wait, opening one at random, will find something to interest him .

Among the fine furniture in the adjacent, cosy drawing-room is a rare Queen Anne walnut bureau with a toilet mirror above, while its most imposing picture is an 1856 view in oils by Cowen, looking from the terrace of Windsor Castle towards Eton (including, incidentally, the house at which the schoolboy Thomson boarded there, H.E. Luxmoore's) (p. 24).

Beyond the study and the drawing-room is Dorneywood's largest and grandest room, occupying most of the ground floor of the east wing. This is the conference room, previously known as the music room (p. 34, 47). Its grained pine panelling is cornered and intersected with handsome Corinthian pilasters, while the floor is divided by two expansive oriental carpets, which came, in 1988, from 11 Downing Street. At one end there is a bow window overlooking the garden (p. 29); and that is matched, at the other, by an ellipse backed by one of the great

*Oswald Birley's 1937 portrait of Sir Courtauld, which hangs in the hall*

The Calanque Cassis (1920) by Winston S Churchill.
*This oil painting, which was exhibited in the Royal Academy in 1950, was presented by the artist 'as an addition to the gift of Dorneywood to the nation'. The picture hangs in the study*

Dorneywood tapestries and holding a grand piano.

Courtauld Thomson's bagatelle board adds a homely touch to this magnificent apartment. It was the subject of hot competition. There is at Dorneywood a certificate signed by Lord Cherwell, Lord Courtauld-Thomson, Lord Louis Mountbatten and Mr Averell Harriman (U.S. Chief Lend-Lease Officer in London) saying that 'at 4.0 pm on Sunday 6 December 1942, Mr Churchill scored 1015 points at bagatelle in our presence'. The most interesting features of the conference room are its early nineteenth century *trompe l'oeil* (p. 34, to the left of the fireplace) a painting of a glass-fronted cupboard, with - to the right - a real cupboard containing real porcelain and glass objects, an almost exact replica of the *trompe l'oeil*. Seeing photographs of the room when its set of eighteenth-century Venetian blackamoors in gold gesso robes stood there, one cannot help feeling how the conference room must have been that much more impressive in the donor's day. (Alas, those magnificent life-size statues were removed lest they should cause offence to some visitors.)

On the south side of this east wing - accessible from the hall and the drawing-room - is a loggia, or garden room, which, with its simple furniture, has a charming farmhouse air about it. It is where Courtauld Thomson, his sister, Winifred, and their guests often took their meals during the summer months (p. 32).

The house has a total of eleven bedrooms, including six guest rooms with bathrooms, all extremely comfortable and attractive. The wall of the staircase leading to them is decorated with mezzotint engravings of seventeenth-and eighteenth-century historical personalities, pictures of which Courtauld Thomson was, apparently, an ardent collector, for many of these are also distributed in the hall and the passage leading to the cloakroom. The staircase's Chinese fret balustrade circles up to a first-floor landing which tops the Whistler porch. The landing has been filled with what might best be described as a furnished rectangular tent, the ceiling having a silk canopy and the sides curtains which, when drawn back, render it an open room. This 'tent', which is largely a decorative feature, contains a stand on which is displayed the deed of the grant of Courtauld Thomson's barony (p. 9).

Upstairs there are four more portraits of Courtauld Thomson: a youthful head-and-shoulders profile with a fur collar (p. 26) and a large frontal study of him in middle age, wearing a tweed suit; a masterly black crayon sketch by Sargent (p. 31); and another, as a young man, reading a letter. This is by his sister, Winifred, who shared the house with him until her death in the summer of 1944.

What a remarkable woman Winifred Thomson was! Apart from being Courtauld's almost inseparable companion (even when apart they corresponded regularly and always with warm affection) and being responsible for much of the creativity of the house, she contributed several pictures from her own brushes and also a good deal of the needlework. (Having completed her art education in Paris Winifred Thomson specialized in miniatures which were regularly hung in the Royal Academy. She was extremely well read and used to complete *The Times* crossword at breakfast. After others, who were staying in the house, expressed annoyance at finding that the words were already written in she would solve the puzzles in her head without writing a single word. Air Force officers spending their leaves there during the Second World War remembered her with particular affection. There is no doubt that the character and atmosphere of Dorneywood is very much Winifred's as well as Courtauld's.)

Leaving the house, standing with his back to the front door and looking half left across the forecourt the visitor will see an old cart-shed,

*The barn*

*The cottages*

now forming a rustic loggia with, on the near end, a dove-cote. Windows have been let into the back wall of this cart-shed, stained-glass bearing the coats-of-arms of the various institutions with which Courtauld Thomson was associated (p. 42): his prep school, Summerfields; Eton; Magdalen College, Oxford; that of a Bailiff of the Grand Cross of St John; and that of a High Sheriff of Buckinghamshire, along with his family crest. The barn complex adjoining this contains an excellent squash court and a billiards and table-tennis room (p. 39).

Returning to the front door and walking right-handed along the front of the house the visitor will be amused to see a little white door in the wing labelled 'Toad Hall' - named, of course, in honour of Elspeth's husband, the author of *The Wind in the Willows*. Looking left from there is the row of picturesque brick-and-timber staff cottages. Built originally for the farm workers and restored, with great care, by Courtauld Thomson, they are approached by a brick-paved, flower-edged path known as 'the Street' (p. 45).

## THE GARDEN

By purchasing adjacent land whenever it was offered for sale Lord Courtauld-Thomson extended his estate to 250 acres; and, during his time, Dorneywood was very much a working farm (for the most part tenanted). He also established a pleasant, modest garden. Soon after the National Trust took over, the land was tenanted and the garden was further developed. This expansion was somewhat held up by the existence of large trees close to the house and these were gradually removed - more for the safety of the buildings than to give light or for horticultural purposes.

A large orchard was created to the west of the house while - to provide more house plants, and for potting purposes - the greenhouse range was extended. Between that and the house there was an old marl-pit (containing a well, the principal use of which was to serve water to a horse trough). This attractive sunken feature, known as the Dell, was planted up with roses in Courtauld Thomson's time. Then in 1968 the National Trust gardens adviser was asked to provide a design that would make rather more of it. Twenty years later, by which time the majority of the plants (nearly all summer flowering) were well past maturity, it was decided to clear everything in the Dell away, with the exception of two or three ornamental trees, and to replant with an all-round-the-year interest. The Dell's trees now include a weeping cherry (*Prunus subhirtella* 'Pendula Rosea'), a fine weeping willow-leafed pear (*Pyrus saliciifolia* 'Pendula'), a Mount Etna broom (*Genista aetnensis*), and a tall Italian cypress (*Cupressus sempervirens*).

The rose garden (p. 22) which stands just above the Dell and was designed, in 1985, by another adviser to the National Trust, is composed of a number of beds formed into a circular geometric pattern and surrounded by a yew hedge. In bloom the colour is a medley of pink, white and apricot, with 'Peaudouce', 'Yellow Cushion', 'Apricot Silk', 'Grus an Aachen', 'Troika', 'Silver Jubilee' and 'Chanelle'.

Below the south front of the house is a glorious herbaceous border, mainly of purple, pink and blue, and including a smoke bush (*Cotinus coggygria*), Fuchsia (*magellanica Versicolor*), Sedum 'Autumn Joy', Agapanthus 'Headbourne Hybrids', Ceanothus 'Topaz', Penstemon 'Garnet' and Salvia 'Indigo'. From there the lawn sweeps down to the sunken fence, the ha-ha, the eye being drawn southwards over farmland which has the image of parkland.

The swimming-pool is on the west side of the house. Part of the adjacent ground, once occupied by a putting green, was then devoted to a shrubbery. But, in 1990-91, the shrubs were taken out and another lustrous herbaceous border planted, backed by a yew hedge. Between the tennis-court, which lies next to the orchard, and the drive is a tree and shrub garden, reserved, in particular, for species giving strong autumn colours.

In short Dorneywood's is an ideal manor-house garden with plenty of undulation and variety, intimately surrounding the buildings in a quiet farmland setting.

*The byre, showing some of Lord Courtauld-Thomson's stained glass motifs*

*South Front: a view along the terraces*

## SOME RESIDENTS LOOK BACK

'The period during which Dorneywood was placed at my disposal was from March 1974, when I became Foreign Secretary, until April 1976, when I was appointed Prime Minister and inherited Chequers for the period of my office. As Foreign Secretary, I was away so much travelling abroad that I was not able to appreciate Dorneywood as a home to the extent that I was later able to regard Chequers. There was a different atmosphere, as I used Dorneywood very much for official entertainment of foreign and Commonwealth visitors. Unfortunately, it was not staffed for such a purpose which was a great pity, as those who came enjoyed the atmosphere very much.

I particularly remember entertaining the present Foreign Secretary of Germany, Hans-Dietrich Genscher, who was appointed to that post shortly after I became Foreign Secretary and has retained it ever since. I was speaking to him about his visit only a few months ago and he remembers a perfect June Saturday morning when the sun was shining and the roses were blooming. Incidentally, his visit began a friendship that has lasted, and Dorneywood can take the credit for that.

My wife also entertained and she particularly recalls a visit by the wives of the Commonwealth High Commissioners and the Secretary-General of the Commonwealth, Arnold Smith of Canada.

Dorneywood was a haven of peace whenever I was able to use it, and its generous gift to the nation has proved extremely valuable.'

*Lord Callaghan of Cardiff KG, PC*

'I first visited Dorneywood in 1974 when I was Secretary of State for Northern Ireland. The province was at a standstill due to the Ulster Workers' Strike and I had come back to talk to the Prime Minister, Harold Wilson, who was at Chequers.

The Foreign Secretary, James Callaghan, who was then in residence at Dorneywood, asked my wife and me to call on my way through to that meeting.

The Foreign Secretary and I talked about events in the calm of his study. We walked in the gardens and in the woods, without the close, but normally necessary protection from the Special Branch. I had a swim in the pool.

The brief visit settled our view of Dorneywood. A place of calm and restoration., It sums up our more considered view of the house and gardens when we took over as residents shortly after I became Home Secretary in 1976.

A Home Secretary has his immediate problems by the nature of the job but there is also much long-term planning to consider, backed by copious papers. Dorneywood was often used to quietly undertake the reading involved in this process; to be followed by discussion with private secretaries ready to translate ideas into shorter and sharper papers in preparation for policy decisions.

We often invited those with whom I was involved as Home Secretary to come down to dinner. A well-planned and organized dinner party is not only pleasurable but through discussion can open up 'windows of thought' often blocked by office formality.

I can recall the evening when a quartet comprising the then Commissioner of Police for the Metropolis, Sir David McNee, Ivor Richard, our Ambassador at the UN, Peter Archer and myself sang round the piano, accompanied by Isabel McNee.

My wife recalls with particular pleasure our family gatherings; our eldest son's engagement party in that large orientally-furnished sitting-room and the second son's twenty-first birthday celebration spent round the pool on a hot July day.

*The Street*

Overall Dorneywood was a restful place for us both, with thoughtful staff inside and out. The flowers in the greenhouse and the gardens were a constant joy.

We both look back at our weekend stays there as a time of calm and restoration.'

*Rt Hon. Merlyn Rees, PC, MP*

'It is hard to say what is so special about Dorneywood, the smallest of the three ministerial country residences. Yet special it undoubtedly is, with a restful and relaxing atmosphere which quite miraculously enhances the quality of busy ministerial life. At Number Eleven, agreeable though it is, we were always conscious of living in a government building. Dorneywood, by contrast, has a wonderfully private feel about it, partly because so much has been scrupulously kept as that extraordinary magpie, Lord Courtauld-Thomson, left it, and whose eclectic collection gives the house its character; and partly because one is looked after so well by such experienced staff. Indeed, it is rather like living in a five-star country hotel where there are no other guests.

But of course what makes it is the setting: so perfect a blend of nature and the gardener's art, so tranquil, so quintessentially English. Sitting in the loggia sipping coffee (or whatever) of a summer's evening, looking out past the diligently maintained garden to the large well-kept lawn and the cowfields beyond the ha-ha, it is hard to imagine that the hurly-burly of London can be so near. Even harder, perhaps, to recall that Slough, where I cut my political teeth, is only a stone's throw away.'

*Rt Hon. Nigel Lawson, MP*

'Twelve months stay is far from long enough to do justice to Dorneywood. But our entire family had great fun celebrating Christmas there, and we greatly enjoyed all the amenities, from billiards to swimming and tennis.

The garden (not forgetting the apples) was a great joy, of course - not least for "Summit", who found it an ideal launching pad for far-ranging rabbit hunts. My wife relished the mushroom picking and we all appreciated the more general introduction to the Thames valley.

Each member of the Dorneywood establishment went out of their way to look after us all with great kindness. Many thanks to each one of them.'

*Rt Hon. Geoffrey Howe, QC, MP*

'The special individual character of Dorneywood, which marks it out from all the other houses used by Ministers, is its warmth. Not just the physical warmth of the log fire in the drawing-room on a winter day, but the pervasive atmosphere of welcome and comfort that breathes through the whole house.

Thankfully, it is built in brick and roofed with clay tiles - not the cold formality of stone, stucco and slate. The colour of the brick is the house's ruddy complexion, and it welcomes all visitors with a smile. Visitors from all walks of life can relax in its intimate atmosphere for the rooms are not too grand, they are on a human scale. There are spirits in every house and the guardian that presides over Dorneywood inspires friendship and intimacy.

There are so many impressions: the games in the barn where every guest should be made to play; the lovely gardens with the most delicious early blackberries; the bagatelle where players fret to enter the annals and sometimes to question the veracity of their predecessors; the deep, deep comfort of the easy chairs; eggs and bacon in the library; and the long and happy dinners in front of Rex Whistler's romantic panorama. Yes, everyone takes from Dorneywood the happiest memories.

As the generations pass I hope that the spirit, which stems from Courtauld Thomson, survives. Dorneywood is not an institution, it is a home, and there can be no higher praise than that.'

*Rt Hon. Kenneth Baker, MP*

*The conference room*

# Appendix A
## *The Residents*

| | Appointment | Period at Dorneywood |
|---|---|---|
| Sir Anthony Eden | Foreign Secretary | February 1955 to June 1955 |
| The Earl of Home | Foreign Secretary | July 1955 to October 1963 |
| | | June 1970 to February 1974 |
| Patrick Gordon Walker | Foreign Secretary | November 1964 to January 1965 |
| Michael Stewart | Foreign Secretary | February 1965 to August 1966 |
| | | April 1968 to June 1970 |
| George Brown | Foreign Secretary | August 1966 to March 1968 |
| James Callaghan | Foreign Secretary | March 1974 to April 1976 |
| Anthony Crosland | Foreign Secretary | May 1976 to February 1977 |
| Merlyn Rees | Home Secretary | April 1977 to May 1979 |
| Viscount Whitelaw | Home Secretary | June 1979 to February 1988 |
| | Lord President | |
| | Deputy Prime Minister | |
| Nigel Lawson | Chancellor of the Exchequer | March 1988 to August 1989 |
| Sir Geoffrey Howe | Lord President | September 1989 to November 1990 |
| | Deputy Prime Minister | |
| | Leader of the House of Commons | |
| Kenneth Baker | Home Secretary | January 1991 to April 1992 |
| Norman Lamont | Chancellor of the Exchequer | April 1992 |

# Appendix B
## *Lord Courtauld-Thomson's Who's Who Entry at the time of his death*

Courtauld-Thomson, 1st Baron cr 1944; kt cr 1912, CB 1916, b 16 Aug 1865; s. of late Robert William Thomson, of Edinburgh and Stonehaven; assumed by deed poll 1944 surname of Courtauld-Thomson; Educ Eton and Magdalen Coll Oxford (MA); High Sheriff Bucks 1933; JP Bucks; One of HM Lts for City of London, 1950- ; holds hon freedom livery and membership of court of Assistants of Paviors Compy; Knight of Grace Order of St John of Jerusalem (Hospitaller, 1918-33) Bailiff Grand Cross 1944; British Red Cross Commissioner France 1914-15; Chief Commissioner Malta Egypt Italy Macedonia and Near East, 1915-19; attached GHQ Staff BEF Egypt 1916 and Italy 1918 (despatches five times); Vice-patron University College Hospital; Ch K Edward VII's Sanatorium, Midhurst; Vice-Ch Cassel hosp for functional disorders; Govr and member finance committee, Star and Garter Home; Council K Edward VII Hospital fund for London; trustee and member Governing body Whiteley village; trustee, Guild of St George; dir Roy Academy of Music; vice-president K Edward VII Hosp, Windsor; vice-president and member of council Officers Assocn; National Fund for Nurses; Ch Limmer and Trinidad Lake Asphalt Compy; ch Merchant Marine Insurance Compy; formerly ch Employers Liability Assurance Corpn; Dir Cable and Wireless (Holding) Ltd and Ass Compys; dep ch Clerical, Medical and General Life Assurance Society Dir, Holloways Properties; Member, Roy Commission on National Museums and Galleries, 1928-30; Ch, National Council for Mental Hygiene, 1922-26; ch, University College Hospital, 1937-45; Treas University College Hospital, 1937-48; ch Red Cross Sales; D of Gloucester's Red Cross St John Fund 1940-45 Ch Princess Christian's Nursing Home, Windsor, 1920-46; trustee, Red Cross Hospital Library, 1916-46; Officer Legion of Honour Order of the Nile (2nd class), Kt comd Order of St Sava of Servia, Order of St Maurice and St Lazarus of Italy, Grand Officer of Danilo of Montenegro and Nichan Iftikhar; Italian Military Cross with bar; Roumanian Cross of Regina Maria; Italian and Serbian Red Cross Gold Medals.

Presented Dorneywood, contents and endowment, to the nation 1942 for the use of the Prime Minister or, at his nomination, for a Secretary of State.

# Bibliography

Courtauld-Thomson, Lord. Unpublished autobiography. Graphic accounts of childhood and youth and wartime experiences. A most illuminating document, the typescript of which is held at Dorneywood, together with numerous letters and notes in his hand.

Hussey, Christopher. Two illustrated articles published in *Country Life*, 7 Dec '51 and 14 Dec '51 - *Lord Courtauld-Thomson's Gift of Dorneywood, Bucks*, by the celebrated architectural historian.

Grahame, Mrs Kenneth. Letters to Courtauld Thomson from his sister, the wife of the author of *The Wind in the Willows*. Also some reminiscences, all held in the Dorneywood archives.

Hamilton, Elizabeth. *The Illustrious Lady: A Biography of Barbara Villiers, Countess of Castlemaine and Duchess of Cleveland* (Hamish Hamilton 1980). Contains an account of Roger Palmer's marriage to the notorious Restoration courtesan.

Moore, S.T. An unpublished history of the Dorney estate, written in note form in two parts, typed in covers - (1) The Narrative (2) The Evidence. This comprehensive chronology by Susan Moore, a professional historical researcher, is largely concerned with the estate up to the time of Lord Courtauld-Thomson's purchase.

Reed, Michael. *The Buckinghamshire Landscape* (Hodder and Stoughton, 1979). Gives a good description of the organization of the county and its farmland in the early days.

Roche, T.W.E. *A Pineapple for the King* (Phillimore, 1971). An account of the seventeenth-century Palmers' royal connections. Dorney Court boasted the first pineapple to be grown in England. It was presented to Charles II.

Strong, L.A.G. *Courtauld Thomson: A Memoir* (John Murray, 1958). A well-written sketch of the Dorneywood donor's life and career.

Thomson, Winifred. Many letters to her brother and sister, held at Dorneywood.

Also numerous press cuttings covering Courtauld Thomson's life, letters from friends and business associates, invitations, dinner seating plans, etc, also in the Dorneywood archives.

*Printed by Bookbuilders Ltd*